Explore Mount Kilimanjaro

Marangu, Machame and Rongai routes

Jacquetta Megarry

Rucksack Readers

Explore Mount Kilimanjaro: Marangu, Machame and Rongai routes

Third edition published 2005 by Rucksack Readers, Landrick Lodge, Dunblane, FK15 0HY, UK

Telephone 0/+44 1786 824 696

Fax   0/+44 1786 825 090

Website   **www.rucsacs.com**

ISBN 1-898481-23-7

British Library cataloguing in publication data: a catalogue record for this book is available from the British Library.

Designed in Scotland by **WorkHorse** (info@workhorse.co.uk)

The maps in this book were created for the purpose by The Linx of Edinburgh © 2001, 2005

Publisher's note

A hike to extreme altitude involves possible health hazards. These have been explained as clearly as possible, and advice offered on how to minimise them. All information has been checked carefully prior to publication. However, the publisher cannot accept any responsibility for any ill-health or injury, arising directly or indirectly from reading this book. Readers should consult their medical advisor before committing themselves to climbing Mount Kilimanjaro.

Explore Mount Kilimanjaro: contents

Introduction

A journey to Mount Kilimanjaro is an exploration, not merely a climb. For some, the appeal is simple: it is the highest summit on earth that is accessible to any committed walker without technical skills or experience. A mere city-dweller may be able to reach 'the roof of Africa'. This is the allure of the highest free-standing mountain in the world.

However, each walker faces a personal gamble, and the stakes are high: altitude symptoms are unpredictable. No amount of preparation can guarantee success. The only certainty is that everyone who takes up this challenge will reach deeply inside themselves during the ascent.

Reaching the summit is not the only goal: success lies rather in the quality of the attempt. Living a lot closer to nature than normally, you may explore your own motivation and recognise your dependency on others. On return from Kili, whether or not you you summited, you will know more about your strengths and weaknesses, and about your fellow humans, than before.

The natural world of this mountain is fascinating. In a landscape formed by ice and fire, the ascent takes you from tropical rain forest to arctic conditions among the summit glaciers. At sea level such contrasts would be 10,000 km apart. On Kilimanjaro, you walk from equator to pole in a few days.

In temperate latitudes, each season lasts for months. High on Kilimanjaro, winter drives out summer every night. This wild place is full of contrasts and extremes. Plants and animals struggle to survive in severe conditions of drought, arctic cold and blazing sunshine. As you journey backwards in time, life-forms become simpler, species are fewer and survival more precarious.

The mountain rises over three miles above the plain on which it stands, making it an outstanding landmark of East Africa. Your climb on Kilimanjaro may increase your self-awareness and perhaps your self-belief. The three research trips on which this book is based (1999, 2000 and 2004) have been unforgettable landmarks in my personal and professional life.

1 Planning and preparation

What is the best time of year?

Because Kilimanjaro is so near the equator, the midday sun is always nearly overhead and the seasons are not as we know them in higher latitudes. The two rainy seasons run from late March to early June and from November to December. Avoid them if possible, visibility tends to be poor and paths slippery. Late June to October and January to early March are the best months to aim for, but heavy rain, snow and thunderstorms can affect mountains at any time, see the photograph on page 57, taken in the 'dry' season.

Consider also the phase of the moon. You will set off on your summit attempt around midnight, and you may want your trip to overlap with a full moon: see page 61 for a web link. Decide how much preparation time you need (pages 5-12). Choose a reputable tour operator with a good choice of routes, a responsible approach to tourism and flights direct to Kilimanjaro International Airport. From Nairobi you face a long overland transfer and border delays.

Combining it with other activities

The air fare to Tanzania is likely to be a major element of your holiday cost, and many trekkers spend a few weeks in this amazing country. You could consider a game safari, a trip to the spice islands of Zanzibar and Pemba, or a visit to Olduvai Gorge. The most famous National Parks (Serengeti, Tarangire and Ngorongoro) are far away, but Amboseli is just across the border in Kenya. Consider also a warm-up climb on Mount Meru: see page 6.

Giraffe, Arusha National Park

If you have only one day to spare, don't miss the chance of a game drive in Arusha National Park. It has a wide range of animals, including baboon, wild buffalo, colobus monkey, hippopotamus and is famous for its giraffes (Tanzania's national animal). Bird life is spectacular, ranging from flamingos, secretary birds and eagles through hoopoes and plovers to colourful sunbirds and bee-eaters.

Meru's ash cone, from crater rim

Mount Meru

Climb Mount Meru (4566 m) just before Kili, perhaps with a rest day in between, and you will vastly improve your chances of summiting Kili, while reducing your risk of altitude sickness. Meru stands in Arusha National Park, a classic volcanic cone that last erupted in 1893. (A few trekkers climb Mt Kenya (Point Lenana, 4985 m) but it's over 300 km away, and a bigger commitment.) Mount Meru is only 75 km as the crow flies, and you'll see inspiring views of Kili, notably the sun rising behind Uhuru from Socialist Peak. The ascent follows the same pattern as Kili, so this climb makes ideal preparation, mental and physical.

Day	Start	Finish	Comments
1	Momella Gate, 1500 m	Miriakamba Huts	mostly easy ascent (1000 m)
2	Miriakamba Huts, 2570 m	Saddle Huts	option of Little Meru (3820 m) side-trip for late pm
3	Saddle Huts, 3570 m	Saddle Huts	hike to summit (4566 m) scrambling, exposure and a 2 am start
4	Saddle Huts	Momella Gate	descent of 2000 m

Don't be tempted by a 3-day Meru itinerary. Although some (already acclimatised) people do so, it makes an exhausting summit day beginning at 2 am and risks ending after sunset. It is far better to enjoy your descent without time pressure. You sleep in well-maintained huts with toilet blocks nearby, and the three nights at altitude are just what your body needs before Kili.

At first you'll see bushbuck, giraffe, warthog and zebra, and you'll be accompanied by a Park Ranger with an ancient Enfield rifle in case he needs to scare off any elephant or buffalo. On day two you emerge from the tall trees into heather moorland, aiming for the saddle area between Meru and Little Meru, the latter a rewarding side-trip near sunset. Summit day is tough, physically more strenuous than summit day on Kili, and the 'descent' (involving some re-ascent and scrambling) is tiring.

Climbing Meru is not merely for acclimatisation. It's an exhilarating volcanic hike in its own right, with dramatic views of the crater's 1500-metre cliffs and ash cone. In good conditions, the scrambling isn't difficult unless you suffer from vertigo, in which case you may settle for Rhino Point (3800 m) instead. (In icy or windy conditions the terrain can be lethal, and you might not be allowed to continue beyond it anyway.)

Choosing your route

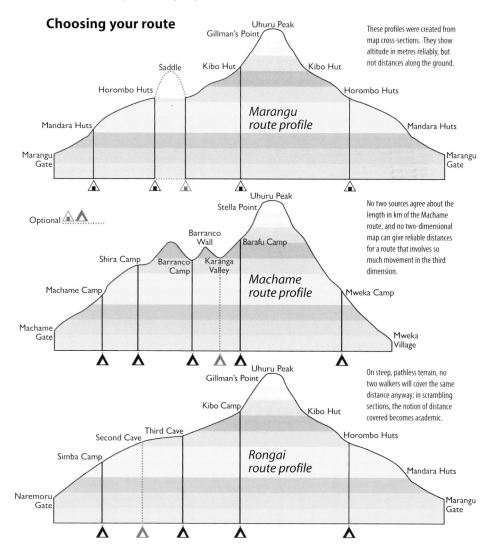

These profiles were created from map cross-sections. They show altitude in metres reliably, but not distances along the ground.

No two sources agree about the length in km of the Machame route, and no two-dimensional map can give reliable distances for a route that involves so much movement in the third dimension.

On steep, pathless terrain, no two walkers will cover the same distance anyway; in scrambling sections, the notion of distance covered becomes academic.

There is a confusing plethora of route names and permutations. This book focuses on the three most popular choices: Marangu, Machame and Rongai, and explains variations such as Lemosho on page 10. For a quick overview, see the route profiles (page 7), Table 1 (page 9) and maps.

Marangu is the original and best-known route, and also the only one where you sleep overnight in bunk-bedded huts with solar-powered electricity. Nearby toilet blocks have running water. Marangu is also known as the 'tourist' or 'Coca-Cola' route, because soft drinks and water are sold. Most huts sleep up to six, except Kibo Hut which has 60 beds in five dormitories. People of either sex are allocated to bunks on arrival, so don't expect privacy. But sleeping in huts is warmer than camping, so if you tend to be cold at nights, Marangu may appeal. It is the cheapest option, and although busy, at least the number of bunks limits overall numbers. Avoid itineraries that offer Marangu as a 3-day ascent. You need an extra night at Horombo for acclimatisation, and you choose how much effort to make next day.

Marangu is the only route on which you return the same way as you ascend. If you prefer variety and don't mind camping, choose Rongai or Machame. You sleep normally two to a tent, relying on your head-torch for lighting. The latrines (toilets) are generally more primitive and further away than on Marangu.

On Rongai, you use Marangu for descent, camping near the huts and making a complete traverse of the mountain. You also have the choice between the direct and indirect alternatives: see page 58. On Machame, you descend by a more direct route, normally via Mweka Camp. It's more strenuous than the other two, because

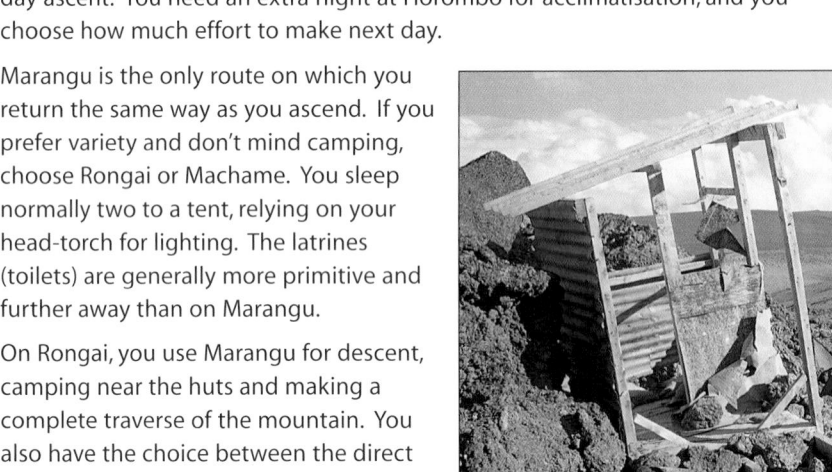

Latrine at Barafu Camp, Machame route

• you walk further, with more ascent and descent
• the terrain is tougher so the hiking takes more effort.

To summarise, if you dislike camping, choose Marangu. Otherwise, choose Rongai, which is both easier and more flexible than Marangu, with more variety and fewer people, albeit with a longer journey before beginning your hike. If you relish the challenge of some easy scrambling and are confident of your fitness, choose Machame. It is the most scenic route, and although it can be crowded, you can avoid most of the crowds by starting your hike mid-week. If you find the choice difficult, read Part 3 carefully and visit our website (see page 61) for links to first-hand diary accounts.

How does route choice affect your chances of summiting? Overall, 'success' rates for Marangu are about 40-50%, although some operators claim 70% or more. The average is depressed by low-budget, minimum-stay tourists who omit the extra night at Horombo, a false economy because so many people suffer altitude sickness as a direct result. Higher percentages are quoted for Machame and Rongai, but this doesn't mean you improve your personal chances by avoiding Marangu. Fit, experienced hikers are attracted to the camping routes, and are more likely to succeed on any route.

The evidence is that exertion is a major risk factor in altitude sickness. If your main aim is to maximise your chance of reaching the summit, choose Rongai or Marangu, which have only one seriously taxing day. On Machame, your summit attempt comes after four strenuous days of trekking, and is immediately followed by a prolonged descent. Reaching the summit, however, is not everything, and there are good reasons why many people prefer the longer, more scenic Machame route, which can be made less tiring if extended by an overnight in Karanga Valley.

Table 1: Summary of routes

Route	Book sections	Map panels	Number of days	Grade*	Comment
Marangu ascent	3·1-3·4	2, 3	5	B	[4 days only if pre-acclimatised]
Machame ascent	3·5-3·9	4	5/6	C/B	the most scenic route; involves some easy scrambling
Rongai ascent	3·10, 3·11a, 3·12a	1	5	A/B	direct route [4 days only if pre-acclimatised]
	3·10, 3·11, 3·12b		5	A/B	indirect route [4 days only if pre-acclimatised]
Descent (all routes)*	3·13	1, 3, 4	1	A/B	all descent is by Marangu or Mweka, with one overnight after summit day descent

* excluding summit day which on all routes is very strenuous (D/E) and includes the first 2000-3000 m of descent

Lonely campsite in the Reusch Crater

Other routes, variations and prices

Other trekking routes include Umbwe, Lemosho and Shira. Umbwe is a tough, steep ascent from the south. It joins the Machame route at Barranco Camp (after an overnight at Cave Camp, 2850 m): see map panel 4. It is much less crowded than Machame, but the altitude gain is too rapid for most people.

The Lemosho and Shira routes approach from the west, starting with a long drive to register at Londorossi Gate. Lemosho is a variation of the seldom-used Shira route on which a 4x4 vehicle drives you to the Shira Plateau at 3500 m. On Lemosho, you take 3 days to walk up from Lemosho Glades (2100 m), via Big Tree Camp (2650 m) and Shira 1 (3600 m), to Shira Camp (3850 m). From there, you follow the Machame options. Lemosho adds a day or two, plus extra travelling and expense, but it's a much less crowded and more varied ascent.

From Barranco Camp, the normal ascent is indirect via Barafu. A challenging variation is to scramble up the Western Breach via Lava Tower (4600 m) and Arrow Glacier Camp (4800 m). This has exposed, steep sections, and after snowfall you'd need crampons and ice axe for the last bit. The Western Breach option may be combined with any Barranco Camp route, but is suitable only for climbers with experience.

A final variation is to visit the Reusch Crater itself (or even, at huge expense, to camp overnight in the crater). There is a faint path from the top of the Western Breach, and in theory it can be reached from Stella or Gillman's Points, but a crater excursion would have to be negotiated ahead of time. In practice, the guides are keen to start the descent as soon as you reach the summit.

Overall, Marangu is the cheapest route, with Rongai/Umbwe next, then Machame, and Shira/Lemosho the most expensive. This mainly reflects the time spent on the mountain, because Park fees and wages are charged per diem. But the longer your trek, the greater your chances of summiting enjoyably.

Fitness, exercise and heart rate

Muscles become stronger if they are used regularly, at a suitable level and for a sustained period. This is known as the training effect. The heart is the most vital muscle to train, so that it can pump blood more efficiently and deliver more oxygen. Your cardiovascular (CV) system – your heart and lungs working together – is severely tested by climbing at altitude.

At sea level, most fit people have a low resting pulse and a high maximum heart rate. Depending on activity level, the heart might beat at any rate between 50 and 200 beats per minute (bpm). At altitude, the resting pulse increases and the maximum reduces, so you climb within a smaller range.

Awareness of heart rate and target zones can help to optimise your training programme. CV fitness improves if you exercise 3-6 times per week for at least half an hour with heart rate in your 'target zone', which is 70-85% of maximum heart rate. As your fitness improves, you have to work harder to push your heart into its target zone. Establishing your target zone and exercising within it is much easier if you use a heart rate monitor (see panel).

People vary widely in their maximum heart rate. Discover your own by experiment if possible. Ignore the well-known tables of zones calculated by an age-related formula. They are unduly cautious for high-altitude trekking, being averaged out for general use. Establish the best target zone for you, given that on summit day your heart may have to work at 130-150 bpm for hours on end. Parker's book explains how best to use monitors in training: see page 61.

Without a monitor, the normal guideline is to work hard enough to make you pant, but not so hard that you cannot also talk. For endurance, it is important to include much longer sessions at least once a week, to prepare your body for the long hours of sustained effort at altitude. You should progressively build up both the duration and difficulty of the sessions.

Heart rate monitors

Monitors have two elements: a chest-worn sensor (on the left), and a wrist-worn display showing heart rate in beats per minute (right). A monitor helps your fitness programme because it tells you objectively how hard your body is working. Its value on the mountain includes monitoring your acclimatisation and helping you to avoid ascending too quickly by raising awareness of how fast your heart is beating. A basic monitor can cost as little as $25 (£15) and is much easier to use than trying to feel your neck pulse while exercising. More advanced monitors let you set target zones, store performance data and design training programmes.

Training programmes differ widely. Most people use hiking, running or cycling as their prime activity. Some experts advocate *cross training* and *interval training*. Cross training involves mixing in another form of exercise, e.g. if your core discipline is running, you might cross-train once a week by cycling or hill walking. Interval training involves varying your effort level sharply every couple of minutes during a single session. You keep challenging your heart to prepare yourself for the varying effort. Some experts suggest a rest day after every training day, others suggest once a week.

Fitness, strength and stamina are all important for climbing Kili. Don't rely on a single form of exercise. The smooth surface of an indoor treadmill does nothing to prepare your leg muscles for climbing loose scree or difficult, steep terrain, perhaps in a strong headwind. Try to include some brisk hill walking or cross-country jogging expeditions in the months and weeks prior to departure.

However you exercise, minimise the risk of straining your muscles by warming up slowly beforehand, cooling down gently afterwards, and stretching. Stretching beforehand reduces the risk of injury. Afterwards, it helps to prevent stiffness the next day. Drink plenty of water before, during and after your sessions.

If you are seriously overweight, you should not contemplate climbing Kili. Surplus fat not only adds to your load, it also increases the demand for oxygen and is a risk factor for AMS. If you need to shed some fat, do so gradually and well ahead of your trip. Your training programme should help, but the target zone for weight loss is lower, ideally 60-70% of maximum heart rate.

Most people will lose weight during the climb, despite the plentiful food, because climbing at altitude demands more calories than you take in. Skinny people should be aware of this potential problem, since body fat helps to insulate from the cold. Hypothermia and frostbite are serious risks.

Start training in good time. If you are already fit, a month of special effort might be enough, but if you are unfit, aim to begin 3-6 months in advance. If you smoke, give it up – or at least suspend it until after your trip.

Stop training a day or two before you leave. If possible, arrange for a spare day on arrival in Tanzania and go for a long walk. Even at only about 1100 m (3300 feet), the village of Moshi gives most visitors an altitude advantage over their homes. A spare day is a wise precaution anyway, since baggage delays are commonplace. When packing, think hard about which items would be most difficult to replace if they were seriously delayed or lost in transit.

Altitude effects

The altitude problem is the shortage of oxygen: as you climb higher, the air gets thinner. At 6000 m (nearly 19,500 ft), atmospheric pressure is about 50% of that at sea level. You might expect to have to breathe twice as fast so as to inspire as much oxygen, but the reality is much worse. The lungs' ability to extract oxygen deteriorates rapidly with altitude – much faster than the decline in oxygen pressure. Furthermore, when climbing at altitude on difficult terrain, the body needs more oxygen anyway.

Your heart is the pump that makes your blood circulate. The lungs load oxygen into your red blood cells for delivery to your muscles and other vital organs. The oxygen demand from your muscles depends on their activity level, but your brain also needs its share. Despite having only 2% of your body weight, your brain needs 15% of its oxygen. If it gets less, judgement declines, control suffers and speech can become confused.

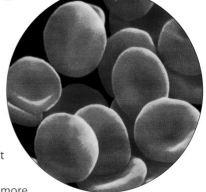

Your body responds in various ways to needing more oxygen:

- you breathe faster and deeper
- your heart beats faster, increasing the oxygen reaching your tissues and forcing blood into parts of your lungs which aren't normally used
- your body expels excess fluid and creates more red blood cells, making the blood thicker.

Red blood cells (greatly magnified)

These changes happen over different time-scales. You start to breathe faster right away. Your heart rate rises within minutes. After several days, your blood starts to thicken. If you find yourself urinating a lot that is a probably a sign that your body is acclimatising well. Creating more red blood cells takes longer still, at least a week, and is irrelevant to most Kili itineraries.

You can help yourself to acclimatise by breathing deeply, and by drinking plenty of water. Sleep is an important time for the body's adjustment: avoid sleeping pills and alcohol, which depress breathing. Standard trekking advice is to limit daily altitude gain to 300 m, but the spacing of campsites on Kili makes that impossible, so acclimatisation is a major issue.

Acute Mountain Sickness (AMS)

Acute Mountain Sickness is the medical term for altitude or mountain sickness, but 'acute' only means 'sudden-onset'. AMS symptoms, if mild or moderate, often disappear if the victim rests or ascends no further. If AMS is severe, the victim must descend: see below.

No expert nor textbook can predict whether or how you will be affected. If you can't face the possibility that you might 'fail' due to AMS, then choose some other mountain. Gender is a factor: females are less likely to experience AMS than males. At moderate altitude, young people are more likely to suffer than their elders: the risk decreases in an almost straight line with age. Individuals vary widely, and even at a given altitude, the same person may be fine one time, yet severely ill another.

> *The author's experience*
> " *On my first ascent (Marangu, 1999) I had almost no symptoms at any altitude, although 7 out of 16 in our group were too unwell to summit. Yet a year later on Machame, I had moderate AMS on the strenuous third day. I recovered overnight to climb a further 2000 metres over the next 24 hours symptom-free. Others in our group first suffered AMS higher up, approaching the crater rim, several so badly that they had to turn back. On a third trip (Rongai, 2004) I was symptom-free, but attribute this to having summited Mt Meru just before.* "

You need to be very fit to climb Kili, but your fitness will not *of itself* reduce your chances of suffering AMS. Over-exertion is a risk factor in AMS, and at a given ascent rate, greater fitness reduces excessive demand for oxygen. In practice, however, ultra-fit individuals are more likely to try to ascend too quickly, thus making themselves more vulnerable.

Complications from AMS (HAPE & HACE)

Edema (or oedema) simply means swelling. HAPE and HACE are High Altitude Pulmonary Edema and High Altitude Cerebral Edema. They are serious complications, caused by swelling of tissues in the lungs and brain respectively. HAPE can occur anywhere above 2500 m and HACE above 3000 m. The risks therefore exist at any time from your first night onward, albeit more probably at higher altitudes, and amongst those who ascend quickly.

HAPE is caused by fluid from tiny blood vessels leaking into the lungs. It affects perhaps 2% of those at altitude, usually people who already have some AMS symptoms. Cold, exercise and dehydration all increase the risk of HAPE. So does gender: males are 5-6 times more likely to be affected than females, and children are more at risk than adults. About 10% of HAPE victims will die unless promptly diagnosed and treated.

The HAPE sufferer typically looks and feels ill, and
- has serious difficulty in breathing, which may be noisy or 'crackly'
- is very weak and cannot sustain exercise
- has a rapid pulse and perhaps a fever
- may have blue-looking lips, ears and fingernail-beds
- has a cough; if there is pink or frothy sputum, the case is serious.

In HACE, swollen blood vessels in the brain cause pressure to build up, causing some or all of: ataxia, dizziness, extreme fatigue, vomiting, acute headache, disorientation, hallucinations, loss of vision, numbness or personality change. Unless treated promptly – by immediate descent, oxygen and suitable drugs – HACE leads to coma and death.

Degrees of AMS

The distinctions between mild, moderate and severe AMS are not watertight, but a useful shortcut is provided by the points system, see Table 2.

Table 2: AMS points

symptom	points	symptom	points	total	degree of AMS	treatment
headache	1	headache (resistant to pain-killers)	2	1-3	mild	drink fluids, pain-killer, rest
insomnia	1	vomiting	2			
nausea or loss of appetite	1	breathing difficulty at rest	3	4-6	moderate	drink fluids, pain-killer, no more ascent until better
dizziness	1	abnormal fatigue	3			
		low urine production	3	7+	severe	immediate descent

Interpretation

Severe AMS can be life-threatening. The victim's judgement is affected and the complications (HAPE and HACE) can be lethal: see the panel on page 14. If you follow good advice, you are very unlikely to experience these, but should know about them. It's ideal if you have a friend along with you, so you can monitor each other's behaviour. Severe AMS is avoidable and treatable, as long as people are aware of its symptoms and take it seriously.

Mild AMS is not uncommon on Kili, but anyone with symptoms should be monitored closely in case they worsen. Assess the sufferer's condition first thing in the morning: symptoms that persist after resting should be taken very seriously. See the panel below for information about Diamox. Many climbers believe that it should be reserved for use as treatment, not prevention. Others prefer herbal alternatives such as ginkgo biloba: there is evidence that this reduces symptoms if started 3-5 days before ascending.

Diamox and AMS

Acetazolamide, known by its trade name of Diamox, has been used as a prescription drug for over 25 years (mainly to treat glaucoma), so it has been studied thoroughly. Opinions differ about its use on mountains: some climbers take it routinely as a preventive measure, but many people argue that this is dangerous because it masks symptoms that are better treated by descent. Many teams carry Diamox with them for use in emergencies because it can help to treat AMS.

When you breathe fast or pant, as when exercising at altitude, you lose a lot of carbon dioxide, reducing the acidity of your blood. Diamox blocks or slows the enzyme involved in converting carbon dioxide. As a result, it speeds up acclimatisation by stopping the blood from becoming too alkaline and smoothing out your breathing.

Diamox has been known to cause severe allergic reactions in a few individuals. If you plan to take it, try it out ahead of your trip to test if you are allergic, to experiment with dosage and to discover whether you can tolerate the side-effects which may include:

- increased urination (diuresis)
- numbness or tingling in hands, feet and face
- nausea
- finding that carbonated drinks taste flat.

Since altitude has a diuretic effect anyway, many people prefer to avoid Diamox, wishing to avoid further interruptions to sleep in order to urinate. Some doctors feel this is a problem only when dosage is too high; individuals vary so much that you will probably have to establish your own level. Taking Diamox makes it especially important to maintain a high fluid intake.

AMS summary

To reduce the risk of AMS:
- ascend slowly and build an extra night at altitude into the itinerary
- drink lots of water
- keep warm, eat regularly and look after yourself.

Be alert for AMS:
- monitor your own and your fellow climbers' acclimatisation
- apply the points system to evaluate symptoms: see Table 2, page 15

If AMS strikes:
- if it is mild, drink more water, rest and take a pain-killer
- if symptoms persist or are more serious, do the above and do not ascend further
- if symptoms are severe or with complications, descend immediately and seek medical help.

"The treatment of altitude-related illness is to stop further ascent and, if symptoms are severe or getting worse, to descend. Oxygen, drugs and other treatments for altitude illness should be viewed as adjuncts to aid descent."

British Medical Journal vol 326, 26.4.2003

"The disorientation crept up on me and I wasn't in any state of mind to diagnose what was going on ... If your mind isn't functioning fully, how will you know that your mind isn't functioning fully?"

From a hiker whose behaviour became erratic at altitude on the Machame route.

Advice on food and drink

Meals are provided and served by support staff. Despite the difficult conditions for preparation and cooking, most people find the food both palatable and plentiful. The diet is rich in carbohydrates, good for helping to overcome altitude symptoms.

Bring some snacks and treats such as dried fruit, trail mix, power bars or high-energy gels. They will boost your energy and morale, and can be shared with others. On summit day, you may be hiking for 15-18 hours, and snacks help to bridge the long gaps between meals. Bring also some throat sweets or peppermints as many people suffer from dry throats at altitude.

Few people carry sufficient water, and even fewer keep it handy. You lose moisture with each breath when walking at altitude, expiring warm moist air and inspiring cold dry air. Also altitude makes your body produce more urine (the diuretic effect), and you lose water vapour all the time, especially when exercising, as invisible sweat. Expect to drink two to four litres per day on top of the liquid you take with meals. If in doubt, check the colour of your urine: pale straw colour is fine, but yellow warns that you are dehydrated.

Try to drink *before* you become thirsty: a water bladder with tube is ideal as it lets you take sips whenever you need, without having to stop or fiddle with rucksacks. Keep iodine purification drops or tablets in your rucksack, and carefully follow the instructions about standing time and dosage in cold conditions. If the flavour bothers you, use neutralising tablets or powder (e.g. Vitamin C). Some people use isotonic powder for an extra boost: added to water, this drink replaces minerals that you lose when sweating.

You can limit your fluid loss through sweating by adjusting your clothing. Try to anticipate your body's heat production. Shed excess layer(s) just before you start to overheat, and restore them just before you start to chill (e.g. for a rest stop or because the weather changes). Because each of these actions means stopping and fiddling with rucksacks, you may prefer to maintain a steady pace and wear clothes designed for flexibility. For example, choose a jacket with underarm zippers and pockets large enough to stow gloves and hat. Trousers with legs that unzip to make shorts help to save weight.

Beyond the last water point, you have to carry all the water you need. On summit day, take care to keep your water bladder or bottle well insulated or close to your body heat; otherwise it may freeze. With bladder systems, the narrow tube is prone to freeze, so either protect it or else after each sip blow back the water to leave the tube empty. Staying well hydrated helps the blood to circulate to your extremities, in addition to warding off AMS.

Food on trek is freshly prepared

Other health issues

A decision to try to walk to extreme altitude carries risks for some people. Before you commit yourself, talk to your doctor. He or she may have no detailed knowledge of altitude physiology so take along your schedule and route profiles (page 7). Unless your medical history involves special risk factors, expect many healthy side-effects from preparing for this trip.

Check the latest information on which vaccinations are required and recommended for Tanzania, and over what timetable. Store your records safely: you may be refused entry without proof of yellow fever protection, for example.

Take advice about anti-malarial drugs and insect repellents, and follow it carefully. Malaria is a life-threatening disease which is easy to prevent but difficult to treat. You need protection, if only for the beginning and end of your trip. If you haven't taken anti-malarials before, ask whether you need to take a trial dose ahead of time. Some can cause side-effects, including nausea and other problems which could be confused with AMS symptoms. You might also want to discuss Diamox.

Remember to visit your dentist well before departure. Your feet are about to become the most important part of your body, so consider seeing a chiropodist, and obtain blister prevention and treatment. If you are a blood donor, make your last donation at least eight weeks before you leave. (Your blood probably won't be welcomed until one year after your return, as AIDS is endemic in this part of Africa.)

Upset digestion is not uncommon, so consider what remedies to take, including anti-diarrhoea medicine. Some of those who have to turn back do so because of diarrhoea and consequent dehydration. The nature of the latrines and absence of running water in most campsites makes it crucial to keep yourself clean. Take a good supply of wet wipes, preferably medicated.

The equatorial sun is very strong, and its radiation more damaging at altitude, so sunburn is a serious risk. Bring a wide-brimmed sun hat, cover-up clothing and cream with a high Sun Protection Factor, at least SPF 33 for your face and lips which are especially at risk. You need wraparound sun-glasses or glacier glasses that block at least 99% of UV radiation, otherwise you risk the pain, headaches and double-vision of 'snow blindness' on summit day. Contact lenses can become very painful to wear at high altitude, so if need be take spectacles for back-up.

Equipment and packing

There is a packing list on page 21. Major items include a well broken-in pair of walking boots, a suitable day rucksack and kit bag, walking poles and a really warm sleeping-bag for the very cold nights at altitude. Be sure to try out anything you buy specially long before you set off.

Everything that isn't in your rucksack will be in your kit bag, which will spend the week being carried on a porter's head. A suitable bag is large, soft and light, without a frame, wheels or dangling straps, not a rucksack or suitcase. Buy or borrow a strong waterproof kit bag or sailing bag/holdall. It should be tough enough to withstand aeroplane baggage handling (or be packed inside something which is). Some tour operators provide kit bags to clients as part of the package.

Trial packing

Long before you depart, do a trial pack to find out if you are within target weight (normally 15 kg/33 lbs). Work through the list on page 21, omitting your hiking boots, which you will either wear or carry as hand baggage. Pack as hand baggage anything fragile (torches, sunglasses, camera) and any medicines you might need during the flight, as well as your passport, ticket, vaccination records and other valuables. Sharp items must be packed in hold baggage.

If your bag is too heavy, try again choosing only the bare necessities. If it weighs under 10 kg/22 lbs, and you have included everything essential, congratulations. Most people will start the climb with between 10 and 15 kg, a bit less once the snacks have been eaten.

Take extra care about packaging and organising: clear polythene zip-lock bags are great for keeping small stuff handy and visible, and cling-film keeps moisture off batteries and other delicate items. Time can be short on the mountain and if you are feeling unwell, easy access makes a big difference.

Before you set off for the trek, you'll be leaving surplus kit and valuables at your hotel. e.g. spare toiletries, a set of clean clothes, aeroplane reading and anything you need for excursions or other parts of your holiday. Although your mountain kit must weigh under 15 kg, you'll be allowed more on the international flight.

Support team numbering two porters per hiker, plus guides

Advice on gear

There is advice on hiking gear on our website (www.rucsacs.com). Even if you don't normally use poles, consider trying or buying them before this trip. They improve your balance, save effort and reduce knee strain, especially on the steep descent. Telescopic poles can be set longer for downhill, shorter for uphill and can be stowed on your rucksack loops, e.g. when scrambling. If you are serious about photography, consider the kind which unscrews to form a camera monopod.

Because of the extremes of temperature, the layer system is vital to control your body temperature. The base should be a 'wicking' fabric, such as knitted polyester. Over that, wear a medium-weight fleece. The outer layer is a waterproof jacket and trousers; choose 'breathable' waterproofs that allow sweat to evaporate. Some people need a down-filled jacket in addition, for cold nights at altitude. Pay special attention to good gloves, footwear and head/face protection, to avoid hypothermia and frostbite.

Don't underestimate how cold you may be at nights, especially on the camping routes. If you can't afford a really warm sleeping-bag and a good sleeping mat, then borrow or hire them. You can't enjoy your holiday if you are too cold to sleep properly. At higher altitudes, some people need to wear most of their clothes at night, including hat and gloves.

Packing checklist

The checklist is divided into *essential* and *desirable*. Experienced trekkers may differ about these categories, but others may appreciate a starting-point. You won't see your main kit bag between morning and night. Carry in your rucksack everything you need for the day's walk. With the exception of the torches, some spare clothing and sleeping gear, that could mean wearing or carrying everything in the *essential* list on most days.

Essential

- well broken-in walking boots
- plenty of suitably warm walking socks
- poles (preferably two for the descent)
- many layers of suitably warm clothing, including underwear
- warm hat and/or balaclava for protection against cold
- broad-brimmed hat for protection against sun
- sun protection for eyes (good quality sunglasses or glacier glasses)
- gloves, glove liners and/or warm mittens (especially for summit day)
- waterproof jacket/trousers
- water carrier(s) (bottles or bladders)
- water purification tablets or drops
- snacks and throat sweets
- first aid kit including blister, headache and diarrhoea relief
- toilet tissue (biodegradable)
- wet wipes and wash bag equipped for cleaning skin and teeth
- head-torch, pocket torch and spare batteries
- sleeping bag rated to -18° to -15°C (0-5°F)
- warm self-inflating sleeping mat (camping routes only)
- enough cash for tips (see page 25) and to buy drinks; US dollars are widely welcomed, but take plenty of small notes as you'll get change in Tanzanian shillings.

Desirable

- light and rugged camera; remember spare batteries and film
- waterproof rucksack cover or waterproof liner, e.g. bin (garbage) bag
- pouch or secure pockets, to keep small items handy but safe
- gaiters (to protect trouser legs on scree and snow)
- thermal liner for sleeping bag
- spare shoes (eg trainers or hut slippers), spare bootlaces
- notebook and pen, playing cards or book
- guidebook and/or map.

Advance planning checklist

This checklist may help you to plan the months prior to departure:

- consult medical advisor about your proposed trip
- take out suitable insurance as soon as you book
- plan and execute training programme for fitness and stamina
- check which inoculations are needed and over what timetable
- visit dentist and/or chiropodist for check-up
- learn some Swahili if possible: see page 61
- weigh all your kit and decide whether to buy or borrow any lightweight upgrades
- blood donors: last donation no less than 8 weeks before departure.

2·1 Tanzania, history and Kilimanjaro's 'discovery'

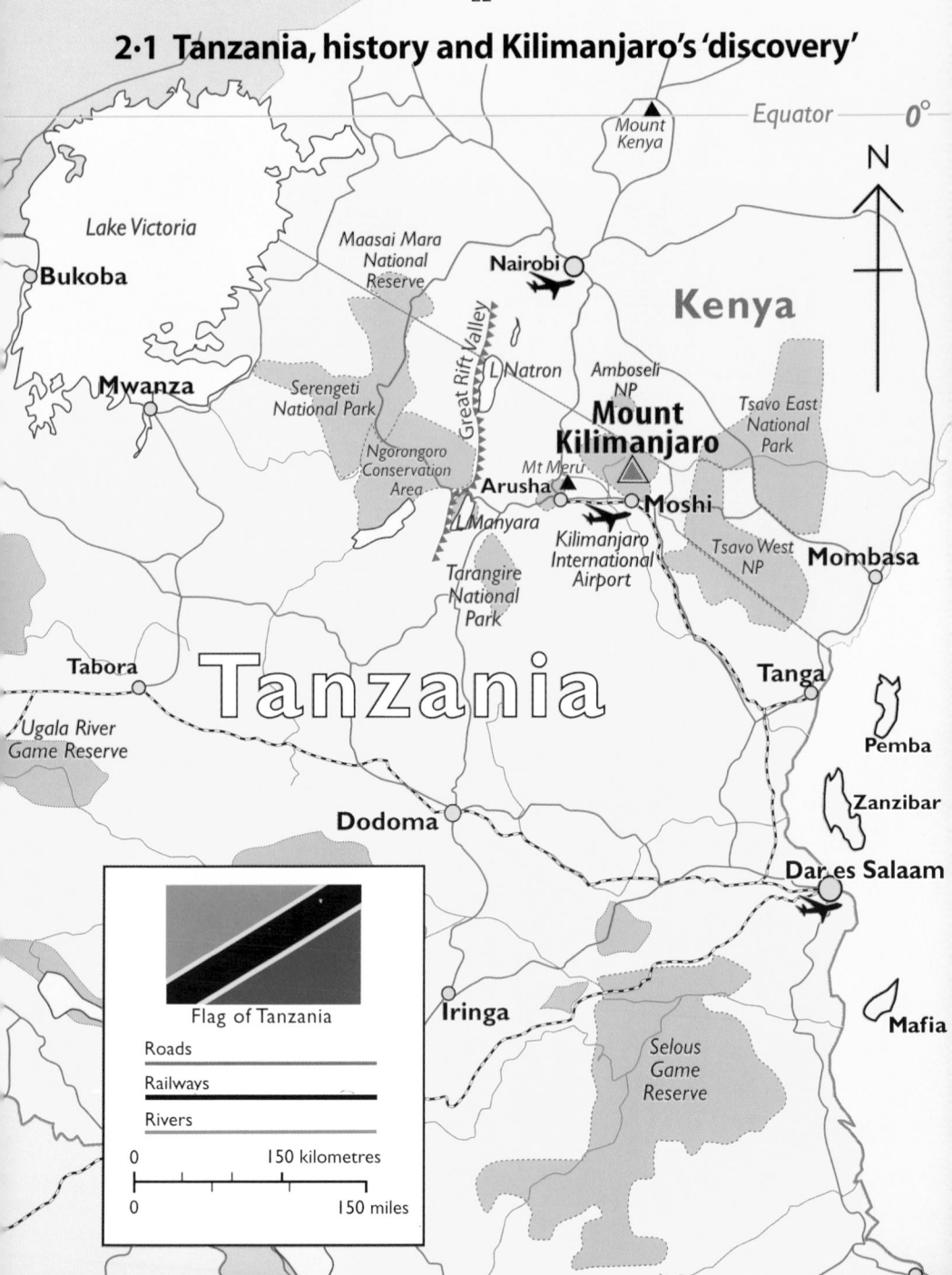

Equator — 0°

N

Mount Kenya

Kenya

Lake Victoria

Bukoba

Maasai Mara National Reserve

Nairobi

L. Natron

Amboseli NP

Tsavo East National Park

Mwanza

Serengeti National Park

Great Rift Valley

Mount Kilimanjaro

Ngorongoro Conservation Area

Mt Meru

Arusha

Moshi

L. Manyara

Kilimanjaro International Airport

Tsavo West NP

Mombasa

Tarangire National Park

Tabora

Tanzania

Tanga

Ugala River Game Reserve

Pemba

Dodoma

Zanzibar

Dar es Salaam

Iringa

Flag of Tanzania

Roads

Railways

Rivers

0   150 kilometres

0   150 miles

Selous Game Reserve

Mafia

Songea

Mtwara

Tanzania is a large country, more than twice the size of California, with many tourist attractions including its Indian Ocean coastal islands and national parks and game reserves covering one-seventh of its area. Its population was about 36.5 million in 2004, with a life expectancy of only 44 years. About 80% of its workforce of 19 million are subsistence farmers. Dar es Salaam is the main port and commercial capital, but the parliament meets at Dodoma which is supposed to become the new capital.

The four colours in its flag symbolise the people (black), the land (green), the sea (blue) and its mineral wealth (gold). Its motto 'Uhuru na umoja' means 'Freedom and unity' in Swahili, the national language. Tanganyika gained independence in 1961, and became the United Republic of Tanzania when it joined with Zanzibar in 1964. Julius Nyerere was its President from 1962-85.

Mount Kilimanjaro is an important national symbol of freedom. The Uhuru Torch was first lit at its summit in 1961, in the words of Nyerere's famous speech, '[to] shine beyond our borders giving hope where there was despair, love where there was hate, and dignity where before there was only humiliation.'

Ptolemy of Alexandria wrote of a 'great snow mountain' in the second century AD, and Kilimanjaro was mentioned by Chinese and Arab writers in the 12th and 13th centuries. However, Europeans were surprisingly slow to 'discover' and accept the idea of a snow-capped mountain only 3° south of the equator.

In 1848, missionary Johann Rebmann, on an expedition to Kilimanjaro, 'observed something remarkably white on the top of a high mountain'. He soon realised that it was snow, and later identified the twin peaks of Kibo and Mawenzi. British armchair geographers refused to believe his first-hand account, published in April 1849 but not accepted for a further 12 years.

Serious attempts by Europeans to climb Kilimanjaro began in 1861, but most groups turned back at the snowline, then as low as 4000 m. Finally, on 5 October 1889, Hans Meyer and Ludwig Purtscheller reached the summit, which they called Kaiser Wilhelm Spitze.

Contrary to a widespread myth, Kilimanjaro was not 'given' by Queen Victoria to her grandson Kaiser Wilhelm. The reason that the line of the border was kinked southward between the mountain and coast was to place the sea port of Mombasa in Kenya, then British. German East Africa (as it then was) kept the port of Dar es Salaam as part of the carve-up of Africa finally agreed by the European powers in Berlin in 1896.

2·2 Conservation, tourism and the local economy

Hotels in Marangu have been running guided ascents of Kili since the 1930s, but numbers were tiny and grew slowly. In 1959, about 700 visitors tried for the summit, of whom around 50% reached Gillman's Point. Numbers increased rapidly through the 1990s, averaging about 20,000 tourists a year since 2000.

All land above 2700 metres is included in Kilimanjaro National Park, and the Park regulations are clearly posted. Walking on this unique mountain carries a responsibility to ensure its preservation for future generations. Your Park fees go towards maintenance of the trails, huts and campsites, helping the authorities to fight a constant battle against woodcutters, poachers, fires and the scourge of litter. As visitors, we can help in a positive way, not only by never leaving litter, but also by picking up the odd piece we may find on the trail. Remember that each person's behaviour acts as an example, good or bad, to others.

Exploitation or economic opportunity?

Especially on a first visit to Africa, many Westerners feel uncomfortable about the idea of 'native porters' carrying their baggage and supplies, preparing meals and putting up and breaking down tents. Porters' loads are up to 18 kg (Marangu/Rongai) or 15 kg (Machame), excluding their personal belongings, whereas the tourist's rucksack probably weighs about 4-6 kg. At one level, this is obviously unfair.

On the other hand, the visitors' holidays pay for the porters' wages and their tips are vital to them and their families. Porters are poorly paid by Western standards, but this is one of the world's poorest countries and they are better off than the unemployed or those in subsistence farming. You will see many would-be porters hanging around the Park gates, competing for this work.

After three years' experience, porters may progress to become Assistant Guides, and after a further year or two, reach the rank of Head Guide. Guides are better paid, normally carry only their own equipment, have some training and speak some English.

Guides and porters are very fit, agile and are mostly well-acclimatised to altitude. But they are human, they also feel tired and may suffer altitude symptoms. Porters may be too frightened of losing their jobs to admit to symptoms, even if they recognise the cause. They also suffer from the cold because of poor equipment. Tragically, there have been several porter deaths from hypothermia and AMS, which could have been avoided with warmer clothing and greater awareness. You can help by expressing concern for a porter who looks cold or ill, and by asking your tour operator (preferably before booking with them) what steps they are taking to ensure fair pay and conditions for porters: see page 61 for links to relevant websites.

Guides are better equipped than porters, but because they have to walk at the slow pace of the visitors, they may also feel very cold. Grateful tourists sometimes donate the odd item of clothing or gear at the end of the trip, and the Guide may operate a system for sharing such extras. Extras are no substitute for fair wages and adequate tips (see panel).

In the Tanzanian context, tipping is not optional, it's a legitimate expectation. Withold or reduce tips only in the very unlikely case of poor service, and spell out what was wrong. Most visitors find the staff very hard-working and polite, and a little ceremony in handing over the tips is customary. Large groups may prefer to hand over the whole kitty to the Head Guide for distribution, but it's more personal if you hand over and thank porters individually.

The Chagga people are one of over 100 Tanzanian tribes, and have lived on and around Kilimanjaro for three or four centuries. Most of the guides and porters are Chagga, many of them from the village of Marangu. They are self-employed, within a framework established by the Tanzanian National Parks, and they have a reputation for independence and strength of purpose. The missionary legacy is surprisingly strong, and most guides and porters seem to be Lutheran; you may even hear Christian hymns sung in Swahili.

Wages and tips: how much?

Different operators pay different rates to their staff, and fierce competition keeps the overall level low. On average, in 2005 the daily wage was (US dollar equivalent) about $3-7 per porter, $4-8 for the cook, $6-9 for Assistant Guides and $9-12 for the Head Guide. However budget operators pay even less than this and there are even rogue outfitters who pay no wages, making porters work for tips alone. If you pay too little for your Kili package, you may be colluding in this shameful practice: try to make amends through tipping. With Park fees of $400-$500 per person, be suspicious of tours that don't cost enough: where margins are tight, the porters' wages will be the first to suffer.

Tour operators normally offer guidance about tipping. If wages are unusually high, lesser tipping might be in order. If service was extra special, be more generous. The amount also depends somewhat on the group size and route. As a general guideline you should allow about 10% of the cost of your tour (excluding air fare) for all the staff, dividing the kitty roughly in proportion to wage rates given above.

2·3 The volcanoes, geology and scenery

The Great Rift Valley reached its present form only between 1 and 2 million years ago. Compared with the formation of the earth around 4000 million years ago, this is, in geological terms, very recent. Long before Kilimanjaro was formed there was a gently rolling plain with the remains of a few eroded mountains. About a million years ago, the plain buckled and slumped, sinking over a period to form a huge basin known as the Kilimanjaro Depression.

The Kilimanjaro of today was formed between 500,000 and 750,000 years ago from three volcanic centres: Kibo was, and still is, the highest at 5895 m, connected by its Saddle region to Mawenzi (5149 m). Shira, at 3962 m, is the oldest and was also the first to collapse and become extinct. Eruptions and lava flow raised Kibo to a height of about 5900 m some 450,000 years ago. Uhuru Peak, Kibo's 'summit', is the highest point of a giant oval crater rim more than 3 km long by 2 km wide. There is no single name for Kilimanjaro in Swahili: its two main peaks are called Kipoo (Kibo) and Kimawenzi (Mawenzi).

The Shira plateau was later worn down by erosion, but it still has interesting minerals (see page 45). Weathering exposed the jagged crags of Mawenzi, formed from slower-cooling, harder rocks that have resisted erosion. Around 100,000 years ago, subsidence caused a huge landslide that breached part of Kibo's crater rim and scoured out the Great Barranco on its way downhill.

Kibo continued to be active, and even today it is technically dormant rather than extinct. Its most violent eruptions were around 350,000 years ago, producing lava flows up to 50 metres thick. This distinctive black lava filled in the Shira basin and flowed over the Saddle area towards Mawenzi.

Kibo viewed from the west, with parasitic cones in left foreground

Later volcanic activity on Kibo formed a smaller crater inside the main one, now known as the Reusch Crater. Over 200 years ago, the last volcanic puff formed the concentric Ash Pit inside it. There are still traces of volcanic activity there, but very few tours include a visit to the crater.

Snow-covered Reusch Crater (c. 1990)

Kilimanjaro's extraordinary scenery was formed not only by volcanic fire, but also by ice. The ebb and flow of the glaciers has modified the shape of the mountain over hundreds of thousands of years. In extreme glacial times, an unbroken sheet of ice covered the entire mountain down to around 4000 m, with finger glaciers reaching down to the tree line at 3000 m.

You might expect that the overhead sun's rays would melt the glaciers, but in fact the flat, white ice reflects most of the radiation. Instead, the dark, dull lava and rocks absorb the heat, and the warm ground undermines the ice cliffs above, creating overhangs and undercuts. As ice blocks fall off and columns splinter, they create shade and help the ground to absorb further heat, melting more ice. You can hear the cracking sounds clearly if you walk past the summit glaciers in suitable conditions.

Kibo's glaciers are in retreat

Sadly, Kibo is gradually losing its ice cap. Compare the upper photograph on page 27 with the one below, and note the snow levels recorded in early expeditions. Although global warming may also have a role, geologists confirm that Kilimanjaro has a long history of glacial advance and retreat. At times it has been completely ice-free for tens of thousands of years, perhaps because of volcanic activity as well as climatic change. At other times, the ice cover has been so complete that ascent would have been impossible. Some predictions suggest the glaciers will be gone by 2020 or even sooner, so enjoy the extraordinary beauty of the summit glaciers while you still can.

Zebra Rock

In the Saddle area you may notice a number of 'parasitic cones': these are small conical hills formed by offshoots of the main lava flow (see photographs on pages 26 and 37). If you do the Saddle walk, you will pass Zebra Rock above Horombo, an overhung cliff face marked by light stripes. These were caused by rainwater seeping down the rock-face from above, leaving light deposits on the dark lava.

On the Machame route, you camp on the Shira Plateau, where there are also many parasitic cones. You will see the Shira Ridge rising 400 m above the main plateau, with dramatic peaks known as the Cathedral and the Needle. Later you see wonderful views of the Lava Tower and Western Breach Wall, and you walk through the Great Barranco.

Aerial view of Mawenzi (foreground) and Kibo (distance) from the southeast

2·4 Habitats and wildlife

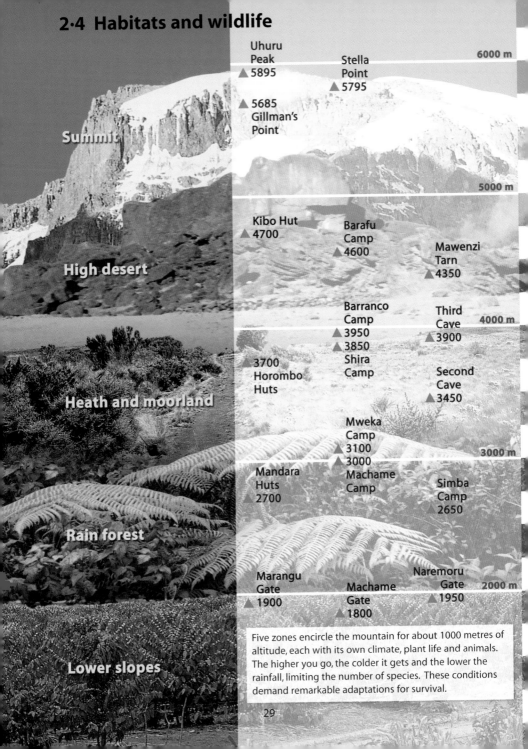

Summit

High desert

Heath and moorland

Rain forest

Lower slopes

Uhuru Peak ▲ 5895

Stella Point ▲ 5795

▲ 5685 Gillman's Point

6000 m

5000 m

Kibo Hut ▲ 4700

Barafu Camp ▲ 4600

Mawenzi Tarn ▲ 4350

Barranco Camp ▲ 3950

Third Cave ▲ 3900

4000 m

▲ 3850

3700 Horombo Huts

Shira Camp

Second Cave ▲ 3450

Mweka Camp ▲ 3100

3000

3000 m

Mandara Huts 2700

Machame Camp

Simba Camp 2650

Marangu Gate ▲ 1900

Naremoru Gate ▲ 1950

2000 m

Machame Gate ▲ 1800

Five zones encircle the mountain for about 1000 metres of altitude, each with its own climate, plant life and animals. The higher you go, the colder it gets and the lower the rainfall, limiting the number of species. These conditions demand remarkable adaptations for survival.

29

The lower slopes

Between about 800-1800 m, the Chagga people cultivate the rich volcanic soil for crops such as maize, coffee and bananas. The south and west sides of the mountain are wetter and more fertile, with rainfall varying from 500-1800 mm (20-70 in) per year. There are brilliant wild flowers and interesting vegetation supporting a wide range of bird life, including the common bulbul (brown with a black crest), the tropical boubou (a black and white shrike), lots of brown speckled mousebirds and nectar-feeding sunbirds (long curved bills and iridescent feathers).

Rain forest

Blue monkey

The rain forest occurs between about 1800-2800 m, with rainfall of about 2000 mm (80 in) per year on the southern slopes. The west and north are much drier, and on the Rongai route the rain forest is sparser and less luxuriant. The forest often has a band of clouds, with mist and high humidity. Fine tall trees are decked with streamers of bearded lichen. Mosses and giant ferns flourish in these conditions, and wild flowers include violets, the occasional orchid and the unique red-and-yellow *Impatiens kilimanjari*, found nowhere else in the world.

Common huge trees include *Podocarpus milanjianus* (with narrow curling leaves, see page 42) and camphorwoods. An oddity is the lack of bamboo, which occurs in the upper belt of rain forest elsewhere in East Africa. In the upper forest, you start to see giant heather trees with yellow-flowered *hypericum* (St John's Wort) growing among them. *Protea kilimandscharica* is common around Maundi Crater and above Mandara, and, as its name implies, is unique to the mountain.

Protea kilimandscharica

Fruit trees attract many birds: if you hear a bird braying like a donkey, it is probably a silver-cheeked hornbill. If you are lucky enough to see a large bird flashing crimson at its wings, it could be a turaco. Most animals are shy and easily hidden in the thick vegetation. You will probably see monkeys in the forest: blue monkeys (actually a dark bluish-grey) and colobus (black with a flowing white mane of hair and thick white tail).

Colobus monkey

Heath and moorland

Between 2800-4000 m are overlapping zones of heath and moorland, with rainfall ranging from 1300 mm (50 in) per year on the lower slopes to 500 mm (20 in) higher up. Frost forms at night, and intense sunshine makes for high daytime temperatures.

Heather and allied shrubs are well adapted to these conditions, the giant heathers (*Erica arborea*) having tiny leaves and thick trunks and grow to 3 metres high. In the upper forest, they grow even taller. You will also see red-hot pokers (*Kniphofia thomsonii*) standing to attention, and colourful *Helichrysums* – clumps of everlasting daisy-like flowers: see page 37.

The moorland is dominated by giant groundsels (senecios and lobelias), especially near water courses. The most striking is *Senecio kilimanjari*, which grows up to 6 metres tall. The smaller *Lobelia deckenii* (up to 3 metres) has a hollow stem and spiralling 'leaves' that close over at night. Look carefully inside and you will see blue flowers sheltering inside their protection.

Senecio kilimanjari (giant groundsel)

Kniphofia thomsonii

Lobelia deckenii

The animal you are most likely to see is the tiny, semi-tame four-striped grass mouse (*Rhabdomys pumilio*), which has found its niche around the Horombo huts. Also, if you sit quietly while eating a picnic lunch, you may be approached by the alpine chat (dusky brown with white sides to its tail). From just above the forest upward, you will often see and hear the harsh croak of the white-necked raven, which scavenges successfully from the huts: see the photograph on page 35.

High desert

The montane (high or alpine) desert zone stretches from 4000-5000 m and has low precipitation, less than 250 mm (10 in) a year. Here summer burns every day with mid-day temperatures of 35-40 °C , whilst at night the winter chill bites deeply. Soil is scanty, and what little there is can be affected by *solifluction*: when the ground freezes, it expands and flows, disturbing plant roots. Only the hardiest can survive, such as the long-lived lichens. They flourish without soil, growing directly on the lava rocks. Lichens are a perfect example of *symbiosis*: a close partnership between fungi and algae that allows both to live in a place where neither could survive alone. The fungus provides the medium whilst the algae photosynthesise the food.

The photograph shows two kinds of lichen: the red is growing flat on the rock surface whereas the grey-green dangles from it. At the foot of the rock, a yellow clump of helichrysum shelters in the lee of the rock. The few plants that survive are slow-growing. Any you see are very old indeed, so take care not to damage them.

The summit zone

Higher up, it is colder and drier still, and the slight precipitation (under 100 mm or 4 in per year) falls mainly as snow. This often condenses from clouds sucked

Hardy lichens grow directly on the rock

up from below when air pressure drops because of the warming effect of the sun. There is no liquid water on the surface: it disappears into porous rock or is locked in as ice and snow.

Living things must not only endure the blazing equatorial sun by day, but also arctic conditions by night. Here altitude defies latitude. With deep frosts, fierce winds, scarce moisture and less than 50% of the oxygen available at sea level, the environment is deeply hostile to life of any kind.

The highest flowering plant ever recorded was a small helichrysum in the crater at 5670 m. Animals are very rare, although in 1926 the Lutheran missionary Richard Reusch found and photographed a leopard frozen in the snow. Hemingway immortalised it in his 1938 short story *The Snows of Kilimanjaro*, remarking that 'No one has explained what the leopard was seeking at that altitude'.

The Kersten glacier, seen from the crater rim

Well-drained forest path

3·1 Marangu Gate to Mandara Huts

Marangu

Map	panel 3
Time (average)	3–4 hours
Altitude gained	800 metres (2625 feet)
Terrain	mainly good path, may be muddy and slippery during or after rain
Summary	a gentle introductory half-day walking through the rain forest

After your kit has been loaded, you will be driven to the Marangu Park Gate for paperwok (registering passport numbers and paying park fees). From Moshi the drive takes around 45 minutes, and gains you 800 metres of altitude. Expect the formalities to take an hour or so, although you might be lucky. Try to identify birds, flowers and trees to help pass the time: see Section 2.4. Also, make sure you have enough drinking water for the day and a packed lunch.

When you meet your guides and porters, try to remember their faces and learn their names. They are about to become very important people in your life, and by the end of the week you may think of them as supermen. (As of 2005, all guides and nearly all porters were indeed male.)

Unless conditions are wet, this hike up a recently made trekkers' trail with deep drainage channels can seem deceptively simple. (Avoid the wider 4x4 road which is now mainly used by porters.) Be conscious of altitude and maintain a slow, steady pace to help your body to acclimatise. If walking as a group, you may stop together for lunch at Kisambioni picnic site, or may postpone lunch until you arrive at Mandara Huts.

Normally this walk takes only half a day, leaving plenty of time to visit Maundi Crater, a fine crater just 15 minutes walk from Mandara. The extra effort is rewarded by brilliant wild flowers and superb views of Kibo and Mawenzi.

Mandara Huts; white-necked raven (inset)

Marangu Gate *1900*

Mandara Huts *2700*

35

3·2 Mandara Huts to Horombo Huts

Marangu

Map	**panel 3**
Time (average)	**5-6 hours**
Altitude gained	**1000 metres (3280 feet)**
Terrain	**good footpath with steady gradients**
Summary	**after clearing the forest, you walk across moorland with some great open views**

After an early start, the walk starts emerging from the forest. Soon, notice the parasitic cone of Kifinika Hill on your left and enjoy intermittent views of Mawenzi (ahead to your right) and Kibo (far ahead). The vegetation has changed markedly, and you will probably stop for a picnic lunch at Kambi Ya Taabu, which is well over halfway. You may see the four-striped grass mice, which are keen, skilful scavengers.

If it is clear, you'll be enjoying mountain views for much of this day's walk, on a good path, arriving at Horombo by early to mid-afternoon. Unless you are pre-acclimatised, you should have two nights here, probably in the same hut (but leave your gear stowed tidily, just in case). Dinner, as at Mandara, is served in the communal dining hut by your support team.

Horombo Huts

Clump of helichrysum ('Everlasting')

On your acclimatisation day, the Saddle walk is highly recommended: the views of Kibo and Mawenzi are terrific, the ascent and descent (to 4400 m and back) is just what your body needs, and if you set off early you will still have most of the afternoon free. You will also be able to see Middle Red, West Lava and East Lava Hills, as well as Barafu Camp to the west. However, if you are nursing blisters or other problems you could opt out of the walk, or do it in part to suit your energy level. At the very least, visit Zebra Rock, only a couple of km above Horombo: see page 28.

Saddle area: the path to Gillman's Point is shown in yellow

Mandara Huts 2700

Optional saddle walk

3700 Horombo Huts

3·3 Horombo Huts to Kibo Hut

Map	**panels 2 and 3**
Time (average)	**5-6 hours**
Altitude gained	**1000 metres (3280 feet)**
Terrain	**good path with steady gradients easing across the saddle (middle of the day)**
Summary	**passing through high semi-desert, you see some good views of Mawenzi and Kibo**

Today's walk begins very similar to the Saddle walk that you may have done yesterday, bearing off north-westerly. Approaching the high desert of the Saddle region, notice how the giant groundsel (senecios, see page 31) persist wherever there is a watercourse. Top up your water supplies at the Last Water point (1½ to 2 hours above Horombo Hut). The path steepens, and the landscape becomes even bleaker, as you approach Kibo Hut.

Giant senecios above Horombo

You may arrive at Kibo Hut by early afternoon for a well-earned rest before the major challenge of the night's summit attempt. Make sure that you purify (or buy) plenty of drinking water for the night's walk, and pack it so your body warmth reaches the water, otherwise it will freeze. It's a common mistake to become dehydrated at altitude.

This is also the moment to insert fresh batteries and/or film in your camera and to check or replace your head-torch battery. Pack enough snacks and morale boosters to see you through the night's walking, and arrange your warmest clothing ready for action, including gloves,

Route junction with white-necked raven

hat and thermals. Then put your head down and sleep if you can. If you can't sleep, just relax and think peaceful thoughts: your body needs to rest before the very strenuous 24 hours ahead.

High desert, approaching Kibo Hut, with Mawenzi (background)

3·4 Kibo Hut to the summit

Map	**panel 2**
Time (average)	**6-10 hours**
Altitude gained	**985/1195 metres (3230/3920 feet) to Gillman's Point/ Uhuru**
Terrain	**a steep, rough ascent on loose scree and rocks to the crater rim; gentler gradients thereafter**
Summary	**by far the most strenuous stage of the route, normally attempted between midnight and dawn**

You will be woken around midnight to walk through the night. This is mainly because you need the time to try to reach the summit but still descend in daylight. To reach your next night's accommodation via Uhuru, you need not only to gain 1195 m of vertical height, on a slope averaging some 27%, but also to lose 2195 m (Section 3.13). Also, in some ways walking at night is easier as the scree is firmer when cold or frozen and the snow less slushy in the early morning.

On waking, slip into as many layers of clothing as you have: you will be cold, perhaps very cold, to start with, but may need to shed layers after you have been climbing for a while. Alternatively, if a high wind gets up, you may become colder than ever, especially your hands, feet and ears.

Sunrise behind Mawenzi, summit ascent

Eat and drink whatever is on offer. Check that your drinking water and snacks are handy and that the water will not freeze. When your head-torch is switched on, take care not to dazzle others by looking directly at them. If there is moonlight, you may not need the head-torch.

The first half of this ascent is on a steep, winding rocky path. Try to maintain a very slow, but steady pace, rather than constantly stopping for short pauses. Shorten your stride on steeper scree, and don't be afraid to hang back if the pace is too fast for you. Many people get into a trance-like rhythm, trudging up rhythmically through the starlight. You may have a proper rest at Hans Meyer Cave, which at 5150 m is halfway in altitude to Gillman's Point, but the section above the Cave takes longer because the path becomes steeper as it zig-zags up towards the crater rim.

This is by far the most difficult section of the route, and mental strength is important as Gillman's Point mysteriously never seems to get any closer. Simply plod on and don't be discouraged: if you are determined, and escape altitude sickness, you will get there in the end. Your feet may slip back on the scree: try pushing harder on those poles, and edge in with your boots. As you near or reach the crater rim, the sun will raise your morale and body temperature. Pause to enjoy what many people consider the finest sunrise on earth.

From Gillman's Point, it takes another 1½ to 2 hours to Uhuru Peak, although the gradients are much gentler and the terrain easier. There's no point in making a colossal effort to reach the summit unless you are also still capable of getting yourself down: read Section 3.13 carefully ahead of time. You may find that the achievement of reaching the summit gives you a rush of energy that sees you through this, perhaps the longest day of your life.

Summit glacier seen from crater rim

Kibo
Hut 4700

Gillman's
Point

Uhuru
Peak 5895

Giant tree (Podocarpus milanjianus)

3.5 Machame Gate to Machame Camp

Machame

Map	panel 4
Time (average)	5–7 hours
Altitude gained	1200 metres (3940 feet)
Terrain	rough path with many tree roots; very slippery and muddy when wet
Summary	a straightforward first day, unless wet underfoot, on a path enclosed by rain forest

As with the Marangu route, the day begins with a drive to the park gate (Machame) and the formalities (registering passport numbers and paying park fees) take an hour or so. From Moshi the drive takes about 35 minutes, and it takes you to 1800 metres. Try to identify birds, flowers and trees to help pass the time: see Section 2.4. Also, make sure you have enough drinking water for the day and a packed lunch.

When you meet your guides and porters, try to remember their faces and learn their names. They are about to become very important people in your life, and by the end of the week you may think of them as supermen. Because the terrain is rough and sometimes steep, on this route porters occasionally fall. Even with your lighter load and poles for support, you may on occasion struggle for balance, especially if it is wet and muddy underfoot. Spare a thought for the people who are carrying your luggage, tents and cooking equipment.

The walk through the rain forest is full of interest, although it feels curiously enclosed for a mountainside. Mist and cloud are common in the late morning to mid-afternoon, and on arrival at Machame Camp you may see disappointingly little. Early mornings are better for views at this height. Get in the habit of looking around the campsite and locating your torch well before darkness falls.

Machame Camp

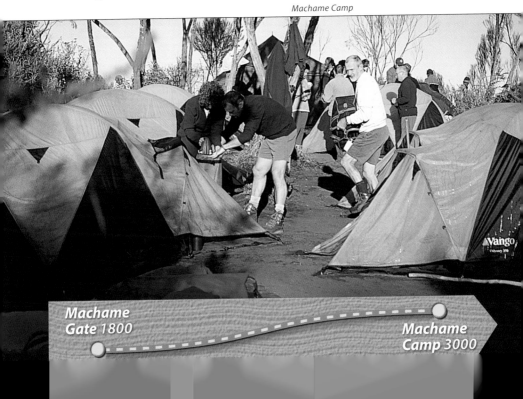

Machame Gate 1800

Machame Camp 3000

3·6 Machame Camp to Shira Camp

Map	**panel 4**
Time (average)	**5-7 hours**
Altitude gained	**850 metres (2790 feet)**
Terrain	**path mostly good with only one real scramble – the rocky ridge leading to Shira plateau**
Summary	**steady climb leads to splendid campsite on Shira plateau**

Scrambling up to Shira plateau

After an early breakfast, you set off toward Shira plateau. Leaving the forest, the path heads up into the moorland along a ridge of volcanic rock. About two hours after Machame, there is a short scramble up a rock 'wall', but this is neither difficult (American Class 3, British grade 1) nor high (about 8 metres). The path climbs steadily along the ridge towards a picnic lunch stop, usually at around 3600 m.

Once you have completed the rocky ridge, you head north, apparently away from Kibo. After crossing some streams, you emerge on to Shira plateau, where the gradients ease and you pass Shira Cave. Shira is the oldest of the three volcanoes that make up the Kilimanjaro massif, and its plateau has many interesting features and minerals. You may notice shiny jet black pebbles lying on the ground, made of obsidian.

Continuing north, you soon reach the first of the three campsites. From here you may have splendid views of the Shira Ridge to the west, with its three pinnacles of Shira Needle, Shira Cathedral and East Shira Hill. Looking east, you may see Kibo's Western Breach and its glaciers. Far away, to the south west, you might even see Mount Meru: see page 6.

Shira Camp

Machame Camp 3000

Shira Camp 3850

3·7 Shira Camp to Barranco Camp

Map	panel 4
Time (average)	5–6 hours
Altitude gained	rising 680 metres (2230 feet) above Shira before steep descent to camp (100 m/330 ft net gain)
Terrain	fairly rough path, some scree, some steep sections
Summary	through rocky semi-desert with dramatic views of the Lava Tower and Breach Wall

From above Shira Camp, looking east

From Shira, your route turns sharply east, and at last you are walking directly toward Kibo and its Western Breach. The line of nearby hills to the left of Kibo is the Oehler Ridge. You climb steadily to a high point of 4530 m, close to the distinctive Lava Tower. There are impressive cliffs and rock formations all the way, with some interesting colours if the light is good.

The last few hours of the day are spent descending steeply into the Great Barranco (valley), ending at an altitude of 3950 m, only 100 m higher than your starting-point. Nevertheless, you will have climbed and descended 680 m (2230 ft) and may be ready for

Breaking up Shira Camp

a hard-earned night's sleep. First, take time to enjoy the spectacular situation of Barranco Camp, which lies below the Western Breach. The front cover photograph shows its tents in the foreground; look closely, and you will see that the white of the clouds differs from that of the snows.

Lava Tower

Shira Camp 3850

Barranco Camp 3950

3·8 Barranco Camp to Barafu Camp

Map	**panel 4**
Time (average)	**7–8 hours**
Altitude gained	**rises 380 metres (1250 feet) over the Barranco Wall, then falls and rises to Barafu (650 m/2130 ft net gain)**
Terrain	**after a steep, exposed climb up the Barranco Wall (some scrambling), gradients ease**
Summary	**a taxing day, to be followed by an even tougher night, but with good views**

From the campsite, you head north for a short distance and cross a river before meeting the day's main challenge: the imposing-looking Barranco Wall. Although the Wall is close to vertical in places, your route takes a diagonal line and is not as hard as it appears at first. The scrambling itself is no more difficult than on Day One, but it is more exposed and lasts much longer – a stiff climb of over 300 metres. You will feel a great sense of achievement looking down from the top.

If you aren't used to scrambling, follow behind someone who is, putting your hands where he or she does: your feet will follow. If you are worried by the exposure, don't look down. Think of the Wall as a long, uneven staircase with handholds. It's amazing to watch the porters calmly walk up carrying heavy weights on their heads, without using their hands.

Porters ascending the Barranco Wall

After the Wall, the path crosses a plateau area divided by several valleys with superb views up towards the southern icefields – in the order that you see them, they are the Heim, Kersten and Decken glaciers. You descend fairly steeply into the Karanga Valley (4000 m), the last water point, so before leaving stock up with water for Barafu and beyond. Most groups stop for lunch here, important fuel for the night-time attempt on the summit, but some add a day to the standard itinerary and camp here overnight.

Hot lunch, Karanga Valley

About 3 km after the Karanga Valley, the circuit path meets the Mweka trail, which is the normal Machame descent route. You turn left at this junction, heading up toward Barafu Camp. Alternatively, your group may take a more diagonal route from Karanga Valley, in effect cutting the corner to reach Barafu. Once you are settled in, watch out for lovely evening light on Mawenzi: the photograph on page 58 was taken here near sunset.

As the campsite is exposed and rocky, it is especially important to familiarise yourself with the terrain before dark falls. There have been a number of accidents at Barafu over the years, mainly at night. Read also page 39 for reminders on checking your gear before nightfall.

Rocky descent towards Karanga Valley

Barranco Camp 3950 — Barranco Wall — Karanga Valley — **Barafu Camp 4600**

3·9 Barafu Camp to the summit

Machame	
Map	panel 4
Time (average)	6–10 hours
Altitude gained	1195/1295 metres (3920/4250 feet) to Stella Point/Uhuru
Terrain	a steep, rough ascent on loose scree and rocks to the crater rim; more gradual thereafter
Summary	the most strenuous stage of a strenuous route, normally attempted between midnight and dawn

As on the Marangu route, you will be woken around midnight to walk through the night, and you need the early start to try to reach the summit and still have time to descend in daylight. To reach your next night's accommodation via Uhuru, you need not only to gain 1295 m of vertical height, but also to lose 2795 m (see Section 3.13). Read pages 40–41 for advice on preparation.

Approaching Stella Point, past the Rebmann glacier

The climb to Stella Point is the most daunting section of the Machame route, mainly because of the altitude and darkness, but there are no technical difficulties. It is a long, steep slog, very steep in places, but if you are determined and escape altitude sickness, you will get there in the end. If your feet slip back on the scree, try pushing harder on those poles and edge in with your boots; watch the guides. As you near or reach Stella Point, the sunrise will raise your morale and body temperature: see the photograph on page 40.

From Stella Point it takes another 45 minutes or so to Uhuru Peak, although the gradients are much gentler and the terrain easier. There's no point in making a superhuman effort to reach the summit unless you are also still capable of getting yourself down: read Section 3.13 carefully ahead of time. However, you may find that the achievement of reaching the summit gives you a rush of energy that sees you through this, perhaps the longest day of your life.

3·10 Naremoru Gate to Simba Camp

Map	**panel 1**
Time (average)	**2½–4 hours**
Altitude gained	**700 metres**
Grade	**mostly easy, with slightly steeper moorland section**
Terrain	**good path with no difficulties**
Summary	**a delightful first day, with great views over the plains of Kenya to the north and towards Kibo**

From Moshi, you will be driven anti-clockwise around the base of Kili's massif for about four hours, mainly on a rough dirt road, passing through scattered Chagga villages. You have plenty of chances to observe the fertile output of the mountain's zone of cultivation. Your journey will probably be extended by an hour or more to deal with Park formalities at Marangu Gate en route. Reaching the village of Tarekea, the road approaches the Kenyan border closely and briefly runs alongside it. Finally, 10 km beyond Tarekea, you arrive at the shanty village of Naremoru (1950 m) and can begin your hike.

First you walk up through lush plantations of maize and potatoes, interspersed with pine and cypress saplings: timber is processed in a sawmill which you pass. The timber shacks are temporary buildings used by the tenant families whose precarious living depends on farming of these fields. Higher up, the path ascends into a band of rain-forest, rich in exotic bird life such as the malachite sunbird and green-and-scarlet turaco. Here you may also hear or see troupes of colobus monkeys (see page 31). Soon you reach an official rest stop with picnic table and toilet.

Fireball lily

Rongai and other names

The Rongai route has many names: trail-side signage refers to Nalemuru or Naremoru, after the village at its foot, or Nare Moru after the river that the trail criss-crosses. Older maps show Loitokitok (after a nearby Kenyan village) or Outward Bound (after the school movement that once used it). The original route started further north at Rongai village, but once the shorter and better Naremoru route was developed, the older route was closed, and transferred its Rongai name to the newer one. Note also that some operators call the first camp Rongai Cave or First Cave, after a cave that (on the original route) marked the first camp. Since there is no nearby cave, we prefer the name Simba Camp.

View north from below Simba Camp

Before long, the trees thin out and give way to open moorland, studded with wild flowers. Because of lower rainfall on the northern side of Kili, the band of rainforest is much smaller than you meet on your Marangu descent. The path now threads its way more steeply among the giant heathers, with wide open views over the plains of Kenya behind you. Soon you reach Simba Camp (2650 m), with its secluded pitches, fine views of peaceful Kibo to your right and jagged Mawenzi to your left. There is fresh water from the Nare Moru river nearby.

Over Naremoru village

Naremoru Gate 1950

Simba Camp 2650

3·11 Simba Camp to Third Cave

Map	**panel 1**
Time (average)	**5–7 hours**
Altitude gained	**1250 metres**
Grade	**mostly easy, with some moderately steep sections**
Terrain	**good path, with no technical difficulties**
Summary	**a sustained hike, with subtle changes in the vegetation and glimpses of Mawenzi and Kibo from different angles; direct and indirect routes diverge at Second Cave**

From Simba Camp you climb mostly gently on a narrow path through the moorland, with some fine open views over Kenya to the north. As you climb, the trees become sparser and later disappear; even the heathers start to shrink at higher altitudes. However, there is still plenty of interest in the wild flowers: the unique *Protea Kilimandscharica* (see page 30), the elegant scarlet *Gladiolus Watsonioides*, and the prickly thistle *Carduus Keniensis*.

You will also see signs of animal life, notably buffalo dung. Eland, the largest of the antelopes, also visit, venturing higher up to the saddle area: you may see their spoor but would be lucky to see these shy animals. Bird life includes the white-necked raven (page 35), the very tame alpine chat (dusky brown with white-sided straight tail) and the streaky seed-eater (a sparrow-like bird with a strong eye-stripe and pale underside). You will probably see the four-striped grass mouse around your camp here.

Simba Camp

Within three hours the path passes First Cave: see photograph below. After a further 20 minutes of rocky path and tussock grasses you reach Second Cave (3450 m). You have gained 800 m of altitude since Simba Camp, and this makes a good lunch stop. Indeed groups with six days to spend may camp there, postponing the further 450 m climb to the next day, or, to save the effort of making and breaking camp, may continue and spend two nights at Third Cave. (Sleeping in caves is prohibited by the National Park, and is unsafe. In the past, they were used by porters for shelter and cooking, but fire damage has weakened the rock ceilings.)

The path to Third Cave leaves from behind and above Second Cave. It's rocky at first, but not too steep, followed by softer ground and then large boulders, with views of Kibo and Mawenzi. The vegetation is thinning out markedly, dominated by low heathers, groundsel and helichrysum (see page 37). The ground is visibly arid, with river beds that are dry for most of the year. It takes only a couple of hours to reach Third Cave (3900 m) from Second – unless altitude slows your progress unduly. This is the last chance to collect water, so stock up with all you need, and expect to carry some spare water up to Kibo Camp for communal purposes.

A more interesting choice if you have six days is to follow the indirect route: see page 58. This option affects the whole group, especially the porters, and the decision is normally taken long before you set off. If your group is small enough to be flexible, you could discuss choices with the guide on arrival at Simba Camp.

First Cave

Simba Camp 2650

Second Cave 3450

Third Cave 3900

3·12a Third Cave to Kibo Camp

Map	**panel 1**
Time (average)	**3½–5 hours**
Altitude gained	**800 m to Kibo Camp**
Grade	**mostly easy, with some moderate or slightly steep sections**
Terrain	**good path with no technical difficulties**
Summary	**another day of steady ascent across the bleakly lunar Saddle region**

Make an early start today so that your body has a chance to rest and recover before your midnight departure for the summit. The route makes a steady ascent across the increasingly arid and bleak montane desert, its greys and browns relieved by the odd hardy lichen and lonely, brave clumps of helichrysum clinging to the shelter of big boulders.

About half-way through the hike at altitude 4300 m, the path divides. The main route continues to Kibo Camp, but an alternative bears off right towards School Hut (formerly known as Outward Bound Hut) – a little-used campsite backed by dramatic cliffs. If that is your destination (this will have been decided by

Third cave campsite, with Kibo behind

your guide in advance) it means a slightly longer, steeper ascent today, balanced by a slightly shorter summit day (albeit one that begins with a scramble up the rocks west of the Hut). School Hut is only 50 m higher than Kibo Hut, and the two routes join just above it, so it hardly matters. The rest of this ascent is described on pages 40-41, and the descent reverses the Marangu ascent (pages 34-39).

Tents at Kibo Camp after snowfall

Most groups continue to Kibo Camp, following the trail steadily upward through the rocks and scree. Abruptly, you'll sight Kibo's large hut, perhaps with tents already pitched around it. Here for the first time you will meet large numbers of other hikers, all on the Marangu route, and can compare notes. Nearly all Marangu hikers will be sleeping dormitory-style in Kibo Hut, rather than camping. (On summit day, everybody descends straight past Kibo Hut down to Horombo, so the folk you meet here are all on their way up.)

Bleak terrain approaching Kibo Camp

Third Cave 3900

Kibo Camp 4700

3·12b Simba Camp to Kibo Camp (indirect)

Day	Start	Finish	Altitude gain m	ft	Time (hrs)
1	Naremoru Gate	Simba Camp	700	2300	2½-4
2	Simba Camp	Kikelewa Caves	950	3120	6-8
3	Kikelewa Caves	Mawenzi Tarn Camp	750	2460	3-5
4	Mawenzi Tarn Camp	Kibo Camp	350	1150	4-6

The alternative route follows two sides of a triangle, taking in Mawenzi Tarn: see map panel 1. It diverges from the direct route at Second Cave (3450 m), which is normally the Day 2 lunch stop: see page 55. Instead of heading south for Third Cave, you bear left (south-east) to camp at Kikelewa Caves (3600 m). You spend your third night at Mawenzi Tarn Camp (4350 m), named after the only tarn (lake) on the mountain. This unique campsite lies right under the jagged features of Mawenzi, with fine views of its northern amphitheatre. This route offers an even better altitude profile than the direct route, and the modest altitude gain on Day 4 is helpful immediately before your summit attempt.

Saving a day

If you are pre-acclimatised and short of time, you could compress the first three days into two, camping first at Second Cave (a gain of 1500 m above the Gate), then Mawenzi Tarn Hut (+900 m) on your second night and Kibo Camp on your third (+350 m).

Jagged peaks of Mawenzi

3·13 The descent

Map	panels 2/3 (Marangu) or panel 4 (Machame/Mweka)
Time (average)	**4-8 hours (including rest/lunch stop)**
Altitude lost	**from Uhuru, 2195 metres (7200 feet) to Horombo Huts or 2795 metres (9170 feet) to Mweka Camp**
Terrain	**gradual descent around crater rim, then steep, loose scree followed by rough path**
Summary	**many people find the descent hard on the knees and feet: don't underestimate this stage**

Coming down sounds simple, and most people underestimate it. On any mountain your chances of falling are greater on the way down, and on Kili's steep scree they are higher than usual. Older walkers will know that descent can be harder than ascent, with potential damage to knees and toes.

The descent from Uhuru begins immediately after the eerie all-night climb. From the summit, you have to lose 2195 m of altitude to reach Horombo (on Marangu) or 2795 m to reach Mweka (on Machame or Rongai). Even from the crater rim, it's 1985 or 2695 m respectively. These are massive descents, much further than you would attempt anywhere else. You have to perform this immediately after a night of enormous effort at high altitude, without a proper rest, let alone sleep.

Then there's the terrain: descending the steep scree is tricky, although using two poles helps. The guides have a nifty technique of half-running, half-sliding down the scree on their heels. Some people find it easy to follow suit, others fall a lot. If you fall, try to relax on the way down and watch out for rocks.

Don't be pressurised into descending faster than you feel safe. The dust may create a serious problem for your eyes, nose and throat, so protect your face. Hold back: it's much worse when you follow another hiker closely.

Campsite at Horombo

Your knees and toes take the brunt of the descent. Start by lacing your boots tightly over the instep, to prevent your toes from hitting the end of the boot. This can cause lasting numbness, especially in the big toe, and may lead to the loss of toenails. If your boots were too short in the first place, you will find this out to your cost.

Once you reach your overnight camp, you'll find beer on sale. Enjoy a couple, but don't go mad: at this altitude, alcohol has about double its effect at sea-level. It is also a diuretic, and may interrupt your night's sleep.

The final day is not described separately. On the Marangu descent, (also used by Rongai) you reverse the two days' climb described on pages 34-37 (1800 m from Horombo to Marangu Gate), with a lunch stop at Mandara Huts. The Mweka descent (used by Machame) is shorter, mainly through the rain forest: 1600 m from Mweka Camp to Mweka Gate (or 1750 m from Rau Camp to Kidia Gate when the longer 'alternative Mweka' or Kidia route is in use).

Your last day on the mountain is precious, and with the pressure off, it seems a shame to hurry it. However, you'll be saying goodbye to the guides and porters at the park gate, and giving them their hard-earned tips. You won't want to delay them unduly before they return to their families. If you are lucky, they may even sing for you – making a lasting memory of an unforgettable week.

4 Reference

Books

Bezruchka, Stephen *Altitude Illness: Prevention and Treatment* The Mountaineers/Cordee 1994 1-871890-57-8

Pocket-sized 93-page coverage of the causes, symptoms and signs, with decision trees, tables, case studies and index; 2nd edition (128 pp) due late 2005 0-898866-85-5

Parker, J L *Heart Monitor Training* 2nd ed Cedarwinds 1993

Scientific approach to optimising training using heart rate data by professional athlete and coach

Pluth, David et al *Kilimanjaro: the Great White Mountain of Africa* Camerapix, Nairobi 2001 1-874041-64-4

This coffee table book has many superb photographs and is good on geology, natural history and the culture of the Maasai and Chagga people. It's an ideal present for Kili aspirants to read ahead of time.

A general guidebook on Tanzania (and perhaps a Swahili phrasebook) would also be useful, e.g. the latest from **Lonely Planet**.

Maps

There are several maps of the mountain, with many discrepancies. EWP's main map (1998) is 1:75,000 but includes useful large-scale of Kibo's summit areas at 1:30,000 and has other maps and drawings inset (0-906227-66-6 www.ewpnet.com). ITM of Vancouver publish in their Mountains of the World series at 1:62,500 (2004 edition 1-553415-53-1). Mark Savage's map is at 1:50,000 (no ISBN but see www.kilimanjaro.com). It's worth buying any of the above in advance of your trip. Locally, the easiest map to find is Hoopoe's colourful but sketchy map of the National Park (about 1:88,000 plus enlarged summit area and background information). There is a parallel map for Arusha National Park (useful for Mt Meru).

Websites

Visit **www.rucsacs.com/books/emk** and click **Links** for links to selected sites including full moon dates and constellations, porter protection, ascent diaries, tour operators' websites, Tanzanian background and photo galleries. To comment on existing links, please email **info@rucsacs.com**.

Get by in Swahili

hello	jambo
goodbye	kwaheri
thank you (very much)	asante (sana)
welcome	karibu
no problem	hakuna matata
sorry	pole
slowly	pole pole
quickly	haraka
let's go (now)	twende (sasa)
yes	ndiyo
no	hapana
danger	hatari
help	usaidizi
toilet	choo
water (drinking)	maji (ya kunywa)
journey	safari
I am tired	nimechoka
my head aches	kichwa kinauma
I feel (much) better	afadhali (sana)
fine, good (very good)	mzuri (sana)
bad	mbaya
hungry	njaa
thirsty	kiu
expensive	ghali
cheap	rahisi
ice, hail	barafu
storm	kipunga
how are things?	habari?
how much/many?	ngapi?
where?	wapi?
when?	lini?
why?	kwa-nini?

Tour operators

Explore Worldwide Ltd pioneered small group adventure holidays, and has run trips to Kilimanjaro since 1993. It arranged the author's first two research trips (Marangu and Machame) through its agent Shah Tours.
Tel: +44/(0) 1252 760 100
website: **www.explore.co.uk**
email: info@exploreworldwide.com

The independent website **www.7summits.com** arranged the third research trip (Mt Meru and Rongai) through its agent Zara Travel. Trips are arranged on a land-only basis to suit travellers from all over the world who have their own flight arrangements. See our Links page for other options.

Visas

Most visitors need a visa for admission to Tanzania. Britons should apply to the Tanzanian High Commission, see website; American citizens should apply to the Tanzanian Embassy in Washington; others should seek advice from their travel agent or tour operator.

Acknowledgements

The author wishes to thank the following people. Many improvements were made as a result of their comments, but any flaws that may remain are our responsibility: Sandra Bardwell, Dr Carol Darwin, Dr Maggie Eisner, Sir Robert Megarry, Caroline Phillips and Brian Spence.

And heartfelt thanks to the porters and guides (above all, Joseph 'Photo' Marandu) without whom the author's ascents would have been far less enjoyable, and perhaps impossible.

Photo credits

Peter Blackwell/BBC Natural History Unit (title page); Nick Anstead (p28 lower), Michèle Cook (p26, p28 upper, p36 and p59), Travers Cox (p27 upper) – all from Explore Worldwide's slide library, reproduced with permission; **Jason Kalbfleisch** p39 upper, p57 upper; **Duncan MacDonald** p10, p17, p47 lower; **Jacquetta Megarry** front cover, p4, p5, p6, p8, p11, p20, p24, p27 lower, p29 all, p30 (both), p31 (lower two), p32, p33 (both), p34, p35 (both), p37 (both), p38, p39 (lower), p41, p42, p43, p44, p45, p46, p47 upper, p48, p49 (both), p50, p51, p52, p53 (both), p54, p55, p56, p57 (lower), p58, p60; **Kristin Reynolds** back cover; **Craig Smith** p40; **www.cellsalive.com** p13.

Rucksack Readers

Uniform with this volume are *Explore the Inca Trail (2002)*, *Explore the Great Wall (2003)* and *Explore the Tour of Mont Blanc (2005)*. We also publish eight books on classic long-distance walks in Scotland and Ireland. For more details, or to order online, please visit **www.rucsacs.com** or telephone +44/0 1786 824 696.

We welcome feedback on this book and on our list: please email us at **info@rucsacs.com**.

ISBN 1-898481-51-2   ISBN 1-898481-20-2   ISBN 1-898481-19-9   ISBN 1-898481-21-0   ISBN 1-898481-22-9

ISBN 1-898481-12-1   ISBN 1-898481-17-2   ISBN 1-898481-24-5   ISBN 1-898481-13-X   ISBN 1-898481-18-0

Index

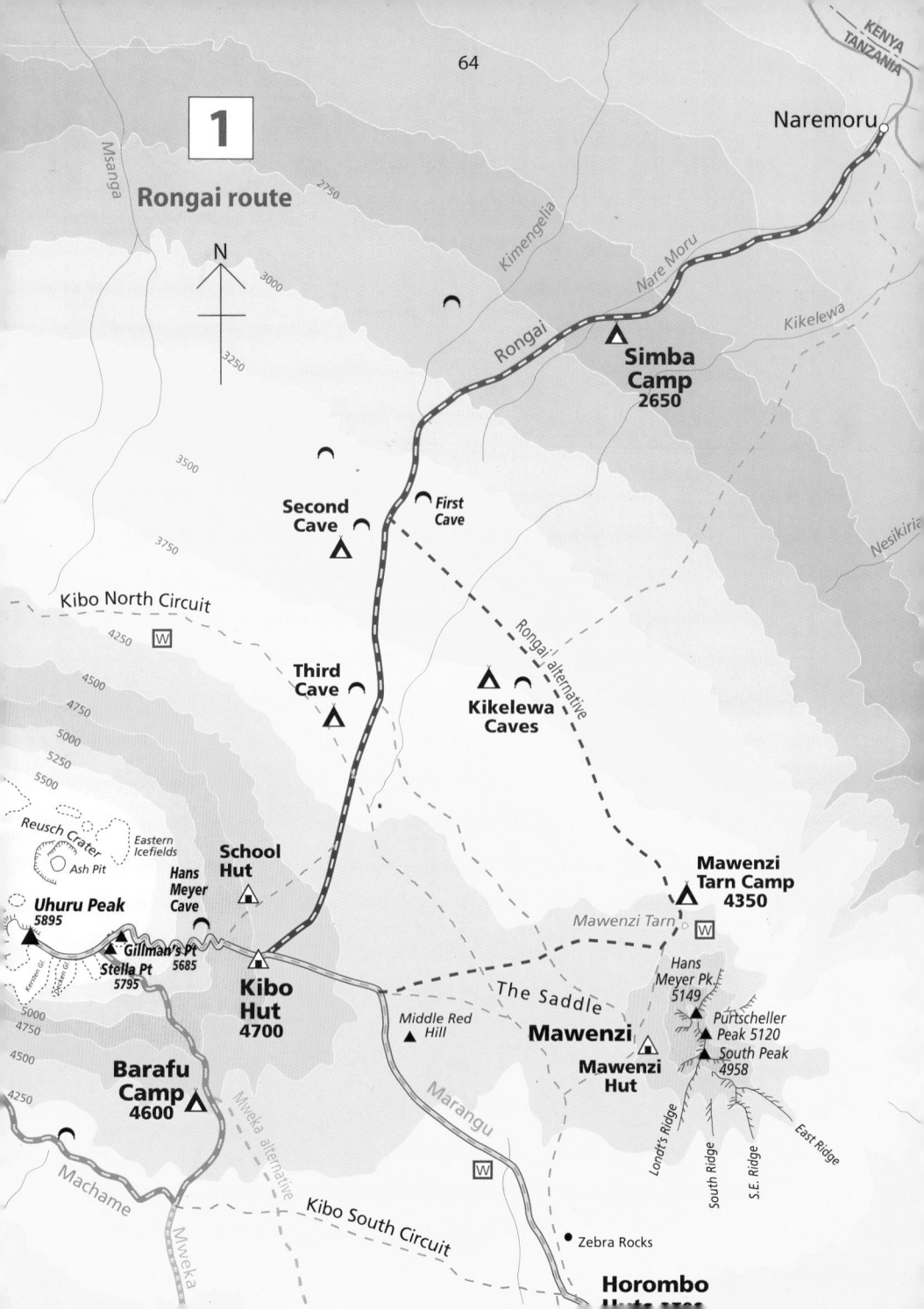

1

Rongai route

N

KENYA
TANZANIA

Naremoru

Simba
Camp
2650

Second
Cave

First
Cave

Kibo North Circuit

W

Third
Cave

Kikelewa
Caves

Rongai alternative

Reusch Crater

Eastern
Icefields

Ash Pit

Mawenzi
Tarn Camp
4350

School
Hut

Hans
Meyer
Cave

Mawenzi Tarn

W

Uhuru Peak
5895

Hans
Meyer Pk.
5149

Gillman's Pt
5685

Purtscheller
Peak 5120

Stella Pt
5795

The Saddle

Kibo
Hut
4700

Middle Red
Hill

Mawenzi

South Peak
4958

Barafu
Camp
4600

Mawenzi
Hut

Londt's Ridge

South Ridge

S.E. Ridge

East Ridge

Mweka alternative

Marangu

W

Machame

Kibo South Circuit

Mweka

Zebra Rocks

Horombo